COLDPLAY
FOR PIANO SOLO

Cover photo credit © Photoshot / Retna Ltd.

ISBN 978-1-4584-3693-1

HAL•LEONARD®
CORPORATION
7777 W. BLUEMOUND RD. P.O. BOX 13819 MILWAUKEE, WI 53213

Visit Hal Leonard Online at
www.halleonard.com

CLOCKS

Words and Music by GUY BERRYMAN,
JON BUCKLAND, WILL CHAMPION
and CHRIS MARTIN

D.S. al Coda
(with repeats)

CODA

FIX YOU

Words and Music by GUY BERRYMAN,
JON BUCKLAND, WILL CHAMPION
and CHRIS MARTIN

IN MY PLACE

Words and Music by GUY BERRYMAN,
JON BUCKLAND, WILL CHAMPION
and CHRIS MARTIN

LOST!

Words and Music by GUY BERRYMAN,
JON BUCKLAND, WILL CHAMPION
and CHRIS MARTIN

Moderately

PARADISE

Words and Music by GUY BERRYMAN,
JON BUCKLAND, WILL CHAMPION,
CHRIS MARTIN and BRIAN ENO

20

D.S. al Coda

CODA

THE SCIENTIST

Words and Music by GUY BERRYMAN,
JON BUCKLAND, WILL CHAMPION
and CHRIS MARTIN

Moderate Ballad

Play 3 times

SPEED OF SOUND

Words and Music by GUY BERRYMAN,
JON BUCKLAND, WILL CHAMPION
and CHRIS MARTIN

Moderately fast

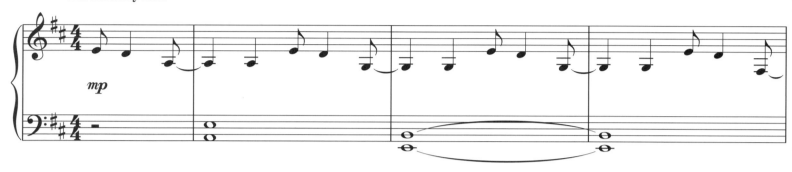

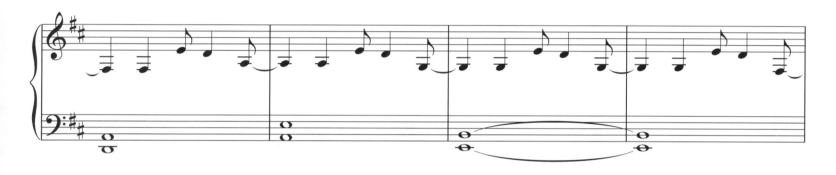

TROUBLE

Words and Music by GUY BERRYMAN,
JON BUCKLAND, WILL CHAMPION
and CHRIS MARTIN

Moderate Ballad

UP IN FLAMES

Words and Music by GUY BERRYMAN,
JON BUCKLAND, WILL CHAMPION
and CHRIS MARTIN

Moderate Ballad

YELLOW

Words and Music by GUY BERRYMAN,
JON BUCKLAND, WILL CHAMPION
and CHRIS MARTIN

VIVA LA VIDA

Words and Music by GUY BERRYMAN,
JON BUCKLAND, WILL CHAMPION
and CHRIS MARTIN

D.S. al Coda

CODA

WHAT IF

Words and Music by GUY BERRYMAN,
JON BUCKLAND, WILL CHAMPION
and CHRIS MARTIN